THE FOOTBALL
COACH
SEASON PLANNER

Bloomsbury Sport
An imprint of Bloomsbury Publishing Plc

50 Bedford Square
London
WC1B 3DP
UK

1385 Broadway
New York
NY 10018
USA

www.bloomsbury.com

First published 2016

© Malcolm Cook, 2016

British Library Cataloguing-in-Publication Data
A catalogue record for this book is available from the British Library.

Library of Congress Cataloguing-in-Publication data has been applied for.

ISBN: PB: 978-1-4729-3394-2

2 4 6 8 10 9 7 5 3 1

Typeset by Mark Silver

THE FOOTBALL COACH
SEASON PLANNER

MALCOLM COOK

BLOOMSBURY
LONDON · OXFORD · NEW YORK · NEW DELHI · SYDNEY

CONTENTS

ENDORSEMENTS

INTRODUCTION   6

    Key Team Factors – Sample   8

    Team Goals for the Season – Sample   9

    Coaching and Training – Sample   10

    Midweek Match/Practice Report – Sample   11

    Weekend Match Report – Sample   12

    Personal Development – Sample   13

    Evaluation – Sample   14

    Team Goals for the Season – Sample   15

PHASE 1: PRE-SEASON   16

    Weeks 1 to 5   18

    Evaluation   34

PHASE 2: PLAYING SEASON   36

    Weeks 6 to 32   38

    Evaluation   146

    Weeks 33 to 42   148

PHASE 3: CLOSE SEASON   188

    Evaluation   190

THE SEASON REVIEW   192

ENDORSEMENTS

'Modern football coaches need to be highly organised and stay ahead of the game by always seeking ways that they can improve themselves. Malcolm Cook's terrific book, *The Football Coach Season Planner* will assist them to do just that. As Director of my natural coaching football Academy, I find the book a great resource for myself and my coaches on our quest to develop our young players and teams to fulfill their potential. The detail inside the book allows coaches to keep up to date with match reports, practice sessions, team meetings, coach performance plus a hundred other important elements. Coaches who use the book will find that they will stay one step ahead of the opposition. I highly recommend the book to coaches at all levels of the game.'

Matthew Le Tissier, former England international and Sky Sports TV presenter

'I have known Malcolm for over ten years. As a highly innovative coach, friend and mentor, I have learned much about the art of football coaching during this time and have been greatly inspired by his work. *The Football Coach Season Planner* is an outstanding coaching tool which is designed to assist the coach to organise, plan and implement all his ideas on and off the practice ground. It has many clever features and I thoroughly recommend it to any coach who wants to take the next step in developing themselves – I know this handy asset won't leave my side.'

Anthony Hudson, New Zealand National Team Coach

INTRODUCTION

Consistency is the most important factor to gaining success. To enable your team to perform well day after day over the season takes attention to detail and cannot be left to chance. This is where *The Football Coach Season Planner comes* in.

ABOUT THE FOOTBALL COACH SEASON PLANNER

It is a combination of diary, motivator and reference that allows you to plan, organize, track and get the best out of your training and coaching programme. In the book, you will find sections to write reports, observations and goals, and record your own and your team's progress throughout the season.

WHY USE THE PLANNER?

Coaches are busy, hard-working people. The Planner will make coaching easier, save time, simplify things and help you be more effective. It will also give you feedback to use and check, monitor and motivate yourself and the team. By regularly reviewing the Planner, you will notice patterns that may need changing, and you can track the team's progress throughout the season and your personal development as well.

> You need passion to spend endless hours developing yourself as a coach. I went on a study tour of England and Brazil to meet coaches. As a coach, if you don't know something you must find the answers, what works and what doesn't – not just in theory but in practice. You must be a student of the game.
>
> **Rafael Benitez**

HOW TO USE YOUR PLANNER

It is specifically designed for football coaches so that you get maximum benefit from it, with appropriate sections and spaces to write in. The season is broken into three specific phases (pre-season; playing season; close season) with room for notes. Some of the features include:

SAMPLE – There are sample copies of all the contents for your guidance.

PERSONAL DEVELOPMENT – As coaches we need to keep progressing, learning and evolving throughout our careers. The Planner has a section exclusively for you as a coach to record your experiences each week, reflect on them later and finally learn the lessons to move on.

QUOTES – There are many from famous coaches to highlight a point, give support or even help to inspire you just when you need it most.

GOALS – There are spaces to set, check and record your season's goals.

EVALUATION – There are a number of evaluation pages where you can do a 'reality check' and provide a clear visual guide of the team's current ability level. This shows you your team's strengths and weaknesses so that you can work on these with your players. Used correctly, it can let you as a coach set accurate goals, give players a realistic benchmark of their level, check progress, improve communication, motivate your team, save valuable training time by focusing on key factors – giving you the edge over other coaches!

Make *The Football Coach Season Planner* your 'assistant coach' that you carry around with you. Its size, design and format make it easily accessible, so get into the habit of writing in notes in each of the sections. There are samples to guide you through, so remember, write soon after each event so that it's still fresh in your memory.

GETTING STARTED

The sooner you make use of this book, the sooner you will improve your coaching and your team. Get off to a head start by writing all the advanced details, dates and information for the season – do it now! (Notice that the first two weeks of the pre-season have no spaces for matches, which should not be played at this time. This helps to avoid injuries before the players are match-fit.)

KEY TEAM FACTORS

1. DISCIPLINE
The team shows self-control under pressure, sticks to the game plan and keeps their 'shape'. We stay together and have a low number of cautions during the season.

2. TECHNICAL
The team are good on the ball and generally 'out-skill' opponents. We have a few outstanding technicians and the team have built a good reputation for skilful football.

3. CONCENTRATION
The team can focus on the game without being distracted. We do our jobs, are aware of helping teammates when needed, and do not make many mistakes over the season.

4. COACHABILITY
The team has a desire to learn and improve. We are receptive to coaching, and show enthusiasm for practice and good relationships with the coaches.

5. TACTICAL
The team shows good 'game understanding' and knows their system of play. We can keep our 'shape' and adapt to different styles and systems of play.

6. LEADERSHIP
The team has experience and players who can take responsibility for their performance. We have a strong captain and other 'leaders' in the team when under pressure.

7. FITNESS
The team always trains hard and is in good physical condition. We can overcome more skilful teams by our sheer work rate and are rarely outmatched physically in games.

8. TEAMWORK
The team trusts, believes and has much confidence in each other and the team. We can 'sacrifice' ourselves for the good of the team and always show camaraderie whatever the result.

9. CONFIDENCE
The team shows respect but no fear of opponents. They believe in themselves, the team and each other. They look forward to taking on teams, especially those with big reputations.

10. DETERMINATION
The team has a great 'will to win' and can bounce back from setbacks. We win games against higher-rate opponents and are always hard to beat.

TEAM GOALS FOR THE SEASON

Write your goals for each season to help you keep focus and remind you of your aims as a coach. Start by writing your goals in the end-of-season section first (see page 15).

(SHORT-TERM)

BY PRE-SEASON	DATE	DONE
1 Check league position.		
2 Check percentage of injuries.		
3 Check goals against.		
4 Check quality of practice.		
5 Check goal attempts averages.		

(MID-TERM)

BY CHRISTMAS	DATE	DONE
1 Check we have at least 20 points to be in at least 10th position.		
2 Devise a better stretching routine to reduce injuries.		
3 Increase defending practice.		
4 Plan more variety in practice.		
5 Increase shooting practice.		

(LONG-TERM)

END OF SEASON	DATE	DONE
1 Finish season in top ten.		
2 Cut down injuries by 20 per cent.		
3 Reduce our goals against by 15 goals.		
4 Ensure quality training over the season.		
5 Create on average 20 finishes on goal per match.		

(Revise any of these goals if required)

Tick ✔ if complete and ✗ if not.

SAMPLE

Football is 10% inspiration and 90% perspiration

GOALS OF THE WEEK

TECHNICAL
Improve our short-passing control techniques and general possession play.

PHYSICAL
Maintain running for endurance plus some extra work on speed, agility and shape.

TACTICAL
Work on movement off the ball to support each other. Deal with high balls at set-plays.

MENTAL
Highlight the need for sharpening up and concentration at start of matches.

TEAM MEETINGS

1. Match inquest on Monday at 9.30 am before training.

2. A meeting with other staff on Friday pm to discuss the team's progress.

MONDAY   3 / 8
Match inquest.
Bright warm-up
Fast passing and ball possession in small games
Some competitive running activities.

TUESDAY   4 / 8
Warm-up

A 2 v 2 practice game (short) conditioned to emphasise team shape, possession and shooting.

WEDNESDAY   5 / 8
Practice match.

THURSDAY   6 / 8
Warm-up with dynamic stretching.

General work in smaller games – Pressing + keeping compact in defence plus possession play.

FRIDAY   7 / 8
Rehearse our team shape/system in a shortened 2 v 2 practice game.

Staff meeting.

SAMPLE

Formation diagram:

1 Wilson

2 Milne | 5 Simpson (Cooper) | 6 Price | 3 Carr

4 Norton | 11 McLean | 8 Nasser

7 Zebec (Reid) | 14 Murray | 10 Dunlop

MATCH DETAILS

V
Second team

DATE
5/08/12

HOME/AWAY
Home

RESULT
3 – 1   (Half time) 1 – 0

COMPETITION
Practice

WEATHER
Cold, windy and wet

PITCH
Narrow and bumpy

SCORERS (Times)
Norton (12 mins)
Price (pen.) (59 mins)
Reid (78 mins)

PLAYERS/TEAM PERFORMANCE

We used this practice match in a game of 2x35 minutes to give the first team a workout versus a mixture of the second team and youth players.

We worked on moving the ball quicker whilst keeping possession. We gave Sam Cooper and Billy Reid a run out and they coped well.

The team also worked on dealing with a number of corner/free-kicks in a 'conditioned' phase of the practice game.

MATCH SUMMARY

The general attitude of the players has been positive. The injuries to 2 key players mean adjustment to the team/system for Saturday's match. We may need to change to a move defensive formation, bring in Cooper or see how our injured players are for the match.

Wilson 1

2 Milne
5 Simpson (Cooper)
6 Price
3 Carr
4 McLean
7 Zebec (Reid)
14 Murray
10 Dunlop
9 Norton
11 Lee

MATCH DETAILS

V
Govan FC

DATE
8/08/12

HOME/AWAY
Home

RESULT
2 – 2   (Half time) 0 – 1

COMPETITION
League

WEATHER
Dry and warm

PITCH
Narrow and bumpy

SCORERS (Times)
Murray (62 mins)
Dunlop (71 mins)

PLAYERS/TEAM PERFORMANCE

We started slowly but gradually found our feet to draw the game versus a strong team.

McLean gave us more solidarity in midfield and helped young Cooper to settle in well.

Simpson covered well for Milne and generally the revisited 4-1-3-2 system worked.

We kept the ball fairly well and missed a couple of chances to win the game. Our fitness came through later when we needed it.

SAMPLE

MATCH SUMMARY

The training and match performance was pretty good overall. Our slow start was a little worrying – we need to sort this out. Cooper and Reid are progressing well and the team spirit is sound. We need to work on dealing with high balls into the box.

Review your performance as a coach during the week

MY COACHING

What went well? <u>*Better communication. Talked less and kept it short and simple. Challenged players more.*</u>

What didn't? Why? <u>*Got into a short argument with a player. Got sucked in when the argument would have naturally run out of steam.*</u>

What would I change next week? <u>*Confrontation! Learn to keep my cool and talk more one-on-one with players.*</u>

HANDLING OF THE MATCH

What went well? <u>*I managed to keep focus, even when we went 0 – 1 down. This allowed me to think more clearly.*</u>

What didn't? Why? <u>*My pre-match talk was rushed and I failed to see how tense the team was.*</u>

What changes would I make next week? <u>*To ensure that I'm in the right state of mind when talking to the team before training and particularly the match.*</u>

IN GENERAL

List 3 positives from this week: <u>*Increased communication. Better awareness and thinking.*</u>

What did I learn about coaching? <u>*Avoid arguments in front of the team. Get myself into best state of mind and plan carefully.*</u>

What did I learn about myself? <u>*That I can change things if I work on them.*</u>

What two things will I work on next week? <u>*Focus on relaxation and working well with my players.*</u>

TEAM REALITY CHECK

PURPOSE

To provide an accurate profile of the team's current abilities.

FACTOR RATING SCALE

DATE ASSESSED __ / __ / ____

KEY FACTORS	VERY LOW 1–2	LOW 3–4	AVERAGE 5–6	HIGH 7–8	VERY HIGH 9–10
1 DISCIPLINE	▓	▓	▓	▓	
2 TECHNICAL	▓	▓	▓		
3 CONCENTRATION	▓	▓	▓	▓	
4 COACHABILITY	▓	▓	▓	▓	▓
5 TACTICAL	▓	▓	▓	▓	
6 LEADERSHIP	▓	▓	▓		
7 FITNESS	▓	▓			
8 TEAMWORK	▓	▓	▓	▓	
9 CONFIDENCE	▓	▓			
10 DETERMINATION	▓	▓	▓	▓	▓

SAMPLE

HOW TO DO IT

1. Read the Key Team Factors (page 8) so you understand them. Rate each one honestly for your own team and mark with a coloured highlighter to produce a visual graph/profile of your team.

2. For more accuracy, get your coaches and/or players to complete a 'team reality check' sheet. Compare the results with your own and discuss differences with them until a score is agreed on.

3. This sample shows that the team have several high factors, a fair average and would benefit from extra work on leadership, fitness and confidence.

4. There are team reality checks at various intervals throughout the year which give you the chance to check your team's progress and maybe change the practice around to improve some factors.

TEAM GOALS FOR THE SEASON

Write your goals for each season to help you keep focus and remind you of your aims as a coach. Start by writing your goals in the 'end of season' section at the bottom.

(SHORT-TERM)

BY PRE-SEASON	DATE	DONE
1		
2		
3		
4		
5		

(MID-TERM)

BY MID SEASON	DATE	DONE
1		
2		
3		
4		
5		

(LONG-TERM)

END OF SEASON	DATE	DONE
1		
2		
3		
4		
5		

Tick ✓ if complete and ✗ if not.

PHASE

1

PRE-SEASON

To win consistently, a team needs a disciplined respect for the coach, its teammates and the fans. Positive results can be achieved by any team in the short term, however, it is only the systematic way they work and practise day by day which allows them to win on a continued basis.

Fabio Capello

PURPOSE

To build a solid foundation of physical fitness, technical skills, tactical understanding, teamwork and psychological readiness for the more intense playing season to come. Follow three stages in this phase to ensure sound progress.

1. GENERAL STAGE

Start gradually in a safe, steady and non-competitive way. This ensures players coming back to training are gently returned to familiar routines of mostly non-football activities such as light training, stretching/body exercises and circuit training to avoid injuries by trying to do too much too soon. (The starting level will depend on the state in which the players return from the close season.)

2. TRANSITION STAGE

There needs to be a progressive and smooth transition from the general activities to work of a more football-specific nature. Trying to jump from one stage to another takes too much adjustment for the players. Ensure the training balance has a 'mix' of running, body exercises allied to ball work, small-sided and functional games, and increased competitive activities and workload.

3. SPECIFIC STAGE

Finally, the work gradually changes to a more energetic, competitive and fast tempo with everything new geared towards the actual game requirements. Coaching now looks to build teamwork, match tactics and systems of play. Training matches versus other clubs are arranged. The objective is to get the team as fully operational as possible for the opening matches of the season, so the team hits the ground running.

The season's journey starts with a single step

GOALS OF THE WEEK

TECHNICAL
_____
_____

PHYSICAL
_____
_____

TACTICAL
_____
_____

MENTAL
_____
_____

TEAM MEETINGS
_____
_____
_____
_____
_____

MONDAY __ / __
_____
_____
_____
_____
_____

TUESDAY __ / __
_____
_____
_____
_____

WEDNESDAY __ / __
_____
_____
_____
_____

THURSDAY __ / __
_____
_____
_____
_____

FRIDAY __ / __
_____
_____
_____
_____

> Review your performance as a coach during the week

MY COACHING

What went well? _____

_____

What didn't? Why? _____

_____

What would I change next week? _____

_____

HANDLING OF THE MATCH

What went well? _____

_____

What didn't? Why? _____

_____

What changes would I make next week? _____

_____

IN GENERAL

List 3 positives from this week: _____

_____

What did I learn about coaching? _____

_____

What did I learn about myself? _____

_____

What two things will I work on next week? _____

_____

*Keep instructions
short and simple*

GOALS OF THE WEEK

TECHNICAL

_____

_____

_____

PHYSICAL

_____

_____

_____

TACTICAL

_____

_____

_____

MENTAL

_____

_____

_____

TEAM MEETINGS

_____

_____

_____

_____

_____

_____

_____

_____

_____

MONDAY __ / __

_____

_____

_____

_____

_____

TUESDAY __ / __

_____

_____

_____

_____

WEDNESDAY __ / __

_____

_____

_____

_____

THURSDAY __ / __

_____

_____

_____

_____

FRIDAY __ / __

_____

_____

_____

_____

> '*We never criticize players – never. We only use two words: "well done." We do this at practice and in the match to build confidence.'*
> Sir Alex Ferguson

MY COACHING

What went well? _____
_____

What didn't? Why? _____
_____

What would I change next week? _____
_____

HANDLING OF THE MATCH

What went well? _____
_____

What didn't? Why? _____
_____

What changes would I make next week? _____
_____

IN GENERAL

List 3 positives from this week: _____
_____

What did I learn about coaching? _____
_____

What did I learn about myself? _____
_____

What two things will I work on next week? _____
_____

*The more you practise,
the luckier you get*

GOALS OF THE WEEK

TECHNICAL

_____

_____

PHYSICAL

_____

_____

TACTICAL

_____

_____

MENTAL

_____

_____

_____

TEAM MEETINGS

_____

_____

_____

_____

_____

_____

_____

MONDAY   __ /__

TUESDAY   __ /__

WEDNESDAY   __ /__

THURSDAY   __ /__

FRIDAY   __ /__

PLAYERS/TEAM PERFORMANCE

MATCH DETAILS

V

DATE

HOME/AWAY

RESULT
_____ (Half time) _____

COMPETITION

WEATHER

PITCH

SCORERS (Times)

MATCH SUMMARY

MATCH DETAILS

V

DATE

HOME/AWAY

RESULT
_____ (Half time) _____

COMPETITION

WEATHER

PITCH

SCORERS (Times)

PLAYERS/TEAM PERFORMANCE

MATCH SUMMARY

> *'My coaching is game-based, where all tactical work is done and discussed in the context of the game.'*
> Roberto Martinez

MY COACHING

What went well? _____

_____

What didn't? Why? _____

_____

What would I change next week? _____

_____

HANDLING OF THE MATCH(ES)

What went well? _____

_____

What didn't? Why? _____

_____

What changes would I make next week? _____

_____

IN GENERAL

List 3 positives from this week: _____

_____

What did I learn about coaching? _____

_____

What did I learn about myself? _____

_____

What two things will I work on next week? _____

_____

*Always finish practice
on a positive note*

GOALS OF THE WEEK

TECHNICAL
_____
_____
_____

PHYSICAL
_____
_____
_____

TACTICAL
_____
_____
_____

MENTAL
_____
_____
_____

TEAM MEETINGS
_____
_____
_____
_____
_____
_____
_____
_____

MONDAY ___ / ___
_____
_____
_____
_____

TUESDAY ___ / ___
_____
_____
_____
_____

WEDNESDAY ___ / ___
_____
_____
_____
_____

THURSDAY ___ / ___
_____
_____
_____
_____

FRIDAY ___ / ___
_____
_____
_____
_____

MATCH DETAILS

V
_____

DATE
_____

HOME/AWAY
_____

RESULT
_____ (Half time) _____

COMPETITION
_____

WEATHER
_____

PITCH
_____

SCORERS (Times)
_____
_____
_____
_____

PLAYERS/TEAM PERFORMANCE

MATCH SUMMARY

MATCH DETAILS

V
_____

DATE
_____

HOME/AWAY
_____

RESULT
_____(Half time)_____

COMPETITION
_____

WEATHER
_____

PITCH
_____

SCORERS (Times)
_____
_____
_____
_____

PLAYERS/TEAM PERFORMANCE

_____
_____
_____
_____
_____
_____
_____
_____
_____
_____
_____
_____
_____
_____
_____
_____
_____

MATCH SUMMARY

_____
_____
_____
_____
_____
_____
_____
_____
_____

> *'As a manager you learn with your ears not with your tongue.'*
> Terry Venables

MY COACHING

What went well? _____

_____

What didn't? Why? _____

_____

What would I change next week? _____

_____

HANDLING OF THE MATCH(ES)

What went well? _____

_____

What didn't? Why? _____

_____

What changes would I make next week? _____

_____

IN GENERAL

List 3 positives from this week: _____

_____

What did I learn about coaching? _____

_____

What did I learn about myself? _____

_____

What two things will I work on next week? _____

_____

Build what you can from where you are, with what you have

GOALS OF THE WEEK

TECHNICAL

_____

_____

_____

PHYSICAL

_____

_____

_____

TACTICAL

_____

_____

_____

MENTAL

_____

_____

_____

TEAM MEETINGS

_____

_____

_____

_____

_____

_____

_____

_____

MONDAY ___ / ___

TUESDAY ___ / ___

WEDNESDAY ___ / ___

THURSDAY ___ / ___

FRIDAY ___ / ___

PLAYERS/TEAM PERFORMANCE

MATCH DETAILS

V

DATE

HOME/AWAY

RESULT
_____(Half time)_____

COMPETITION

WEATHER

PITCH

SCORERS (Times)

MATCH SUMMARY

PLAYERS/TEAM PERFORMANCE

MATCH DETAILS

V

DATE

HOME/AWAY

RESULT
_____ (Half time) _____

COMPETITION

WEATHER

PITCH

SCORERS (Times)

MATCH SUMMARY

> *'As coach, be open to new ideas because the game is always evolving. Be mentally strong because it's a hard job, but always be yourself.'*
> Arsène Wenger

MY COACHING

What went well? _____

_____

What didn't? Why? _____

_____

What would I change next week? _____

_____

HANDLING OF THE MATCH(ES)

What went well? _____

_____

What didn't? Why? _____

_____

What changes would I make next week? _____

_____

IN GENERAL

List 3 positives from this week: _____

_____

What did I learn about coaching? _____

_____

What did I learn about myself? _____

_____

What two things will I work on next week? _____

_____

TEAM REALITY CHECK

PURPOSE

To provide an accurate profile of the team's current abilities.

FACTOR RATING SCALE

DATE ASSESSED __ / __ / ____

KEY FACTORS	VERY LOW 1–2	LOW 3–4	AVERAGE 5–6	HIGH 7–8	VERY HIGH 9–10
1 DISCIPLINE					
2 TECHNICAL					
3 CONCENTRATION					
4 COACHABILITY					
5 TACTICAL					
6 LEADERSHIP					
7 FITNESS					
8 TEAMWORK					
9 CONFIDENCE					
10 DETERMINATION					

HOW TO DO IT

1. Read the Key Team Factors (page 8) so you understand them. Rate each one honestly and mark with a highlighter pen to produce a visual graph/profile of your team.

2. For more accuracy, get your coaches and/or players to complete a 'team reality check' sheet. Compare the results with your own and discuss differences with them until a score is agreed on.

> *We carefully plan our training sessions. For example, suppose we are preparing to play against an aggressive tackling team, we practise quick passing and movement: why? Aggressive players like to tackle a lot and think they are playing well when they do so, so we keep the ball away from them where they can't tackle. They feel they are not contributing to the team so we have them where we want them.*
>
> **Sir Alex Ferguson**

PURPOSE

To break the longest, toughest and most important phase of the season into smaller working periods so that the season will not feel so tough and will help players to avoid becoming stale. Set goals for the players and team to provide focus, motivation and purpose, and regularly re-evaluate everyone before re-setting new goals for the players to reach. There are three important periods during this phase of the season to concentrate on.

1. FIRST HALF OF THE SEASON

(July to September) The early part of the playing season following the pre-season phase is the time to look to get off to a good start. An early defeat is not a disaster, however you are looking to build a sound routine and performance gained from the training/coaching which will transfer into the team's competitive match performance.

2. WINTER PERIOD

(December to January) This period is an important one, with added pressure to play congested matches with little recovery time in between, often in poor weather and playing conditions. The team can pick up injuries to key players, or some players may start to lose focus if points are dropped, but on the positive side, it is an opportunity to attain extra points by winning games in a short period which can move teams up the league.

3. SECOND HALF OF THE SEASON

(April to May) Another period of congested games in the final run-in to the end of the season. Look to build momentum here for the final push to make the play-offs, win the league, gain a promotion place, win a trophy or battle to avoid relegation.

*Always start your practice
with an end in mind*

GOALS OF THE WEEK

TECHNICAL

_____
_____
_____

PHYSICAL

_____
_____
_____

TACTICAL

_____
_____
_____

MENTAL

_____
_____
_____

TEAM MEETINGS

_____
_____
_____
_____
_____
_____
_____
_____

MONDAY   __ / __

_____
_____
_____
_____
_____

TUESDAY   __ / __

_____
_____
_____
_____
_____

WEDNESDAY   __ / __

_____
_____
_____
_____
_____

THURSDAY   __ / __

_____
_____
_____
_____
_____

FRIDAY   __ / __

_____
_____
_____
_____

PLAYERS/TEAM PERFORMANCE

MATCH DETAILS

V

DATE

HOME/AWAY

RESULT
_____ (Half time) _____

COMPETITION

WEATHER

PITCH

SCORERS (Times)

MATCH SUMMARY

MATCH DETAILS

V

DATE

HOME/AWAY

RESULT
_____ (Half time) _____

COMPETITION

WEATHER

PITCH

SCORERS (Times)

PLAYERS/TEAM PERFORMANCE

MATCH SUMMARY

> *'If you practise badly, you get better at playing badly.'*
> Dario Gradi

MY COACHING

What went well? _____
_____

What didn't? Why? _____
_____

What would I change next week? _____
_____

HANDLING OF THE MATCH(ES)

What went well? _____
_____

What didn't? Why? _____
_____

What changes would I make next week? _____
_____

IN GENERAL

List 3 positives from this week: _____
_____

What did I learn about coaching? _____
_____

What did I learn about myself? _____
_____

What two things will I work on next week? _____
_____

If things go wrong:
go back to basics

GOALS OF THE WEEK

TECHNICAL
_____
_____

PHYSICAL
_____
_____

TACTICAL
_____
_____

MENTAL
_____
_____
_____

TEAM MEETINGS
_____
_____
_____
_____
_____
_____
_____

MONDAY __ / __
_____
_____
_____
_____

TUESDAY __ / __
_____
_____
_____

WEDNESDAY __ / __
_____
_____
_____

THURSDAY __ / __
_____
_____
_____

FRIDAY __ / __
_____
_____
_____
_____

PLAYERS/TEAM PERFORMANCE

MATCH DETAILS

V

DATE

HOME/AWAY

RESULT
_____ (Half time) _____

COMPETITION

WEATHER

PITCH

SCORERS (Times)

MATCH SUMMARY

MATCH DETAILS

V

DATE

HOME/AWAY

RESULT
_____(Half time)_____

COMPETITION

WEATHER

PITCH

SCORERS (Times)

PLAYERS/TEAM PERFORMANCE

MATCH SUMMARY

> *'My training as a coach was fully comprehensive.'*
> José Mourinho

MY COACHING

What went well? _____
_____

What didn't? Why? _____
_____

What would I change next week? _____
_____

HANDLING OF THE MATCH(ES)

What went well? _____
_____

What didn't? Why? _____
_____

What changes would I make next week? _____
_____

IN GENERAL

List 3 positives from this week: _____
_____

What did I learn about coaching? _____
_____

What did I learn about myself? _____
_____

What two things will I work on next week? _____
_____

Poor feeding of the ball starves practice

GOALS OF THE WEEK

TECHNICAL

_____
_____
_____

PHYSICAL

_____
_____
_____

TACTICAL

_____
_____
_____

MENTAL

_____
_____
_____

TEAM MEETINGS

_____
_____
_____
_____
_____
_____
_____

MONDAY ___ / ___

_____
_____
_____
_____
_____

TUESDAY ___ / ___

_____
_____
_____
_____

WEDNESDAY ___ / ___

_____
_____
_____
_____

THURSDAY ___ / ___

_____
_____
_____
_____

FRIDAY ___ / ___

_____
_____
_____
_____

PLAYERS/TEAM PERFORMANCE

MATCH DETAILS

V

DATE

HOME/AWAY

RESULT
_____ (Half time) _____

COMPETITION

WEATHER

PITCH

SCORERS (Times)

MATCH SUMMARY

PLAYERS/TEAM PERFORMANCE

MATCH DETAILS

V

DATE

HOME/AWAY

RESULT
_____ (Half time) _____

COMPETITION

WEATHER

PITCH

SCORERS (Times)

MATCH SUMMARY

> 'My coaching is as much about developing the individual player as constructing a winning team. The training is both an education process plus preparing for a specific game.'
> Zico

MY COACHING

What went well? _____
_____

What didn't? Why? _____
_____

What would I change next week? _____
_____

HANDLING OF THE MATCH

What went well? _____
_____

What didn't? Why? _____
_____

What changes would I make next week? _____
_____

IN GENERAL

List 3 positives from this week: _____
_____

What did I learn about coaching? _____
_____

What did I learn about myself? _____
_____

What two things will I work on next week? _____
_____

You have never lost until you quit trying

GOALS OF THE WEEK

TECHNICAL
_____
_____

PHYSICAL
_____
_____

TACTICAL
_____
_____

MENTAL
_____
_____
_____

TEAM MEETINGS
_____
_____
_____
_____
_____
_____

MONDAY __ / __

TUESDAY __ / __

WEDNESDAY __ / __

THURSDAY __ / __

FRIDAY __ / __

MATCH DETAILS

V

DATE

HOME/AWAY

RESULT
_____ (Half time) _____

COMPETITION

WEATHER

PITCH

SCORERS (Times)

PLAYERS/TEAM PERFORMANCE

MATCH SUMMARY

MATCH DETAILS

V

DATE

HOME/AWAY

RESULT
_____ (Half time) _____

COMPETITION

WEATHER

PITCH

SCORERS (Times)

PLAYERS/TEAM PERFORMANCE

MATCH SUMMARY

> *"I am not dealing with footballers,
> I am dealing with people."*
> Pep Guardiola

MY COACHING

What went well? _____
_____

What didn't? Why? _____
_____

What would I change next week? _____
_____

HANDLING OF THE MATCH

What went well? _____
_____

What didn't? Why? _____
_____

What changes would you make next week? _____
_____

IN GENERAL

List 3 positives from this week: _____
_____

What did I learn about coaching? _____
_____

What did I learn about myself? _____
_____

What two things will I work on next week? _____
_____

*Simplicity wins matches,
complexity loses them*

GOALS OF THE WEEK

TECHNICAL

PHYSICAL

TACTICAL

MENTAL

TEAM MEETINGS

MONDAY ___ / ___

TUESDAY ___ / ___

WEDNESDAY ___ / ___

THURSDAY ___ / ___

FRIDAY ___ / ___

PLAYERS/TEAM PERFORMANCE

MATCH DETAILS

V

DATE

HOME/AWAY

RESULT
_____ (Half time) _____

COMPETITION

WEATHER

PITCH

SCORERS (Times)

MATCH SUMMARY

MATCH DETAILS

V
_____

DATE
_____

HOME/AWAY
_____

RESULT
_____ (Half time) _____

COMPETITION
_____

WEATHER
_____

PITCH
_____

SCORERS (Times)
_____
_____
_____
_____

PLAYERS/TEAM PERFORMANCE

_____
_____
_____
_____
_____
_____
_____
_____
_____
_____
_____
_____
_____
_____
_____
_____
_____

MATCH SUMMARY

_____
_____
_____
_____
_____
_____
_____
_____
_____
_____

> 'Coaching must be game-related. The game is the ultimate, so it should be the start and end of practice.'
> José Mourinho

MY COACHING

What went well? _____
_____

What didn't? Why? _____
_____

What would I change next week? _____
_____

HANDLING OF THE MATCH

What went well? _____
_____

What didn't? Why? _____
_____

What changes would I make next week? _____
_____

IN GENERAL

List 3 positives from this week: _____
_____

What did I learn about coaching? _____
_____

What did I learn about myself? _____
_____

What two things will I work on next week? _____
_____

The team is the star

GOALS OF THE WEEK

TECHNICAL

PHYSICAL

TACTICAL

MENTAL

TEAM MEETINGS

MONDAY __ / __

TUESDAY __ / __

WEDNESDAY __ / __

THURSDAY __ / __

FRIDAY __ / __

PLAYERS/TEAM PERFORMANCE

MATCH DETAILS

V

DATE

HOME/AWAY

RESULT
_____ (Half time) _____

COMPETITION

WEATHER

PITCH

SCORERS (Times)

MATCH SUMMARY

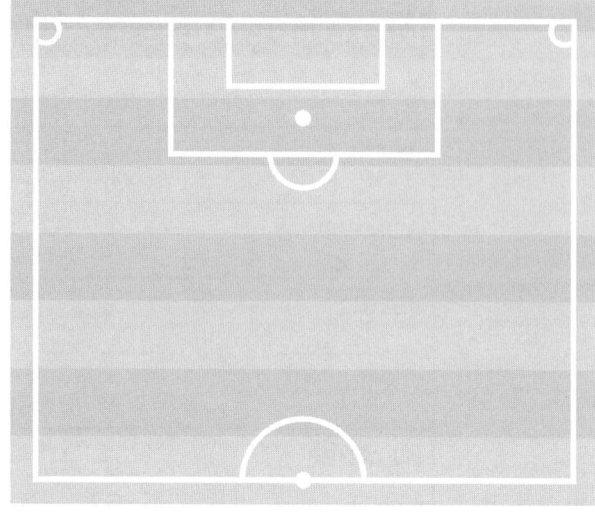

PLAYERS/TEAM PERFORMANCE

MATCH DETAILS

V

DATE

HOME/AWAY

RESULT
_____ (Half time) _____

COMPETITION

WEATHER

PITCH

SCORERS (Times)

MATCH SUMMARY

> 'All Ajax players focus totally during practice sessions.
> They encourage and coach each other to improve.
> They only concentrate on the tactics for 20 minutes
> to give everything, then they change.'
> Rinus Michels

MY COACHING

What went well? _____
_____

What didn't? Why? _____
_____

What would I change next week? _____
_____

HANDLING OF THE MATCH

What went well? _____
_____

What didn't? Why? _____
_____

What changes would I make next week? _____
_____

IN GENERAL

List 3 positives from this week: _____
_____

What did I learn about coaching? _____
_____

What did I learn about myself? _____
_____

What two things will I work on next week? _____
_____

*Good preparation
is power*

GOALS OF THE WEEK

TECHNICAL

PHYSICAL

TACTICAL

MENTAL

TEAM MEETINGS

MONDAY __ / __

TUESDAY __ / __

WEDNESDAY __ / __

THURSDAY __ / __

FRIDAY __ / __

PLAYERS/TEAM PERFORMANCE

MATCH DETAILS

V

DATE

HOME/AWAY

RESULT
_____ (Half time) _____

COMPETITION

WEATHER

PITCH

SCORERS (Times)

MATCH SUMMARY

MATCH DETAILS

V

DATE

HOME/AWAY

RESULT
_____ (Half time) _____

COMPETITION

WEATHER

PITCH

SCORERS (Times)

PLAYERS/TEAM PERFORMANCE

MATCH SUMMARY

> '*I am player-centred in my coaching, and all my decisions as a coach are based on their best interests.*'
> Sammy Lee

MY COACHING

What went well? _____
_____

What didn't? Why? _____
_____

What would I change next week? _____
_____

HANDLING OF THE MATCH

What went well? _____
_____

What didn't? Why? _____
_____

What changes would I make next week? _____
_____

IN GENERAL

List 3 positives from this week: _____
_____

What did I learn about coaching? _____
_____

What did I learn about myself? _____
_____

What two things will I work on next week? _____
_____

Help players to help themselves

GOALS OF THE WEEK

TECHNICAL

PHYSICAL

TACTICAL

MENTAL

TEAM MEETINGS

MONDAY __ / __

TUESDAY __ / __

WEDNESDAY __ / __

THURSDAY __ / __

FRIDAY __ / __

PLAYERS/TEAM PERFORMANCE

MATCH DETAILS

V

DATE

HOME/AWAY

RESULT
_____ (Half time) _____

COMPETITION

WEATHER

PITCH

SCORERS (Times)

MATCH SUMMARY

MATCH DETAILS

V

DATE

HOME/AWAY

RESULT
_____ (Half time) _____

COMPETITION

WEATHER

PITCH

SCORERS (Times)

PLAYERS/TEAM PERFORMANCE

MATCH SUMMARY

'*Train the right way. Help each other. [Football]
is a form of socialism without the politics.*'
Bill Shankly

MY COACHING

What went well? _____
_____

What didn't? Why? _____
_____

What would I change next week? _____
_____

HANDLING OF THE MATCH

What went well? _____
_____

What didn't? Why? _____
_____

What changes would I make next week? _____
_____

IN GENERAL

List 3 positives from this week: _____
_____

What did I learn about coaching? _____
_____

What did I learn about myself? _____
_____

What two things will I work on next week? _____
_____

*Think smarter,
not harder*

GOALS OF THE WEEK

TECHNICAL

_____
_____
_____

PHYSICAL

_____
_____
_____

TACTICAL

_____
_____
_____

MENTAL

_____
_____
_____

TEAM MEETINGS

_____
_____
_____
_____
_____
_____
_____
_____

MONDAY   __ / __

TUESDAY   __ / __

WEDNESDAY   __ / __

THURSDAY   __ / __

FRIDAY   __ / __

MATCH DETAILS

V
_____

DATE
_____

HOME/AWAY
_____

RESULT
_____ (Half time) _____

COMPETITION
_____

WEATHER
_____

PITCH
_____

SCORERS (Times)
_____
_____
_____
_____

PLAYERS/TEAM PERFORMANCE

_____
_____
_____
_____
_____
_____
_____
_____
_____
_____
_____
_____
_____
_____
_____
_____
_____

MATCH SUMMARY

_____
_____
_____
_____
_____
_____
_____
_____
_____
_____

MATCH DETAILS

V

DATE

HOME/AWAY

RESULT
_____ (Half time) _____

COMPETITION

WEATHER

PITCH

SCORERS (Times)

PLAYERS/TEAM PERFORMANCE

MATCH SUMMARY

> *'Coach with simplicity using demonstration to avoid the over-talking trap. You know what's in your mind, but it's not always easy to get it out – best to show rather than tell.'*
> Terry Venables

MY COACHING

What went well? _____
_____

What didn't? Why? _____
_____

What would I change next week? _____
_____

HANDLING OF THE MATCH

What went well? _____
_____

What didn't? Why? _____
_____

What changes would I make next week? _____
_____

IN GENERAL

List 3 positives from this week: _____
_____

What did I learn about coaching? _____
_____

What did I learn about myself? _____
_____

What two things will I work on next week? _____
_____

Somewhere in your difficulties lies opportunity

GOALS OF THE WEEK

TECHNICAL
_____
_____
_____

PHYSICAL
_____
_____
_____

TACTICAL
_____
_____
_____

MENTAL
_____
_____
_____

TEAM MEETINGS
_____
_____
_____
_____
_____
_____
_____

MONDAY ___ / ___
_____
_____
_____
_____
_____

TUESDAY ___ / ___
_____
_____
_____
_____
_____

WEDNESDAY ___ / ___
_____
_____
_____
_____
_____

THURSDAY ___ / ___
_____
_____
_____
_____
_____
_____

FRIDAY ___ / ___
_____
_____
_____
_____
_____

PLAYERS/TEAM PERFORMANCE

MATCH DETAILS

V

DATE

HOME/AWAY

RESULT
_____(Half time)_____

COMPETITION

WEATHER

PITCH

SCORERS (Times)

MATCH SUMMARY

PLAYERS/TEAM PERFORMANCE

MATCH DETAILS

V

DATE

HOME/AWAY

RESULT
_____ (Half time) _____

COMPETITION

WEATHER

PITCH

SCORERS (Times)

MATCH SUMMARY

> *'Coach, before you work on your team,*
> *you first must work on yourself.'*
> John Wooden

MY COACHING

What went well? _____

_____

What didn't? Why? _____

_____

What would I change next week? _____

_____

HANDLING OF THE MATCH(ES)

What went well? _____

_____

What didn't? Why? _____

_____

What changes would I make next week? _____

_____

IN GENERAL

List 3 positives from this week: _____

_____

What did I learn about coaching? _____

_____

What did I learn about myself? _____

_____

What two things will I work on next week? _____

_____

Don't always coach by the book

GOALS OF THE WEEK

TECHNICAL
_____
_____
_____

PHYSICAL
_____
_____
_____

TACTICAL
_____
_____
_____

MENTAL
_____
_____
_____

TEAM MEETINGS
_____
_____
_____
_____
_____
_____
_____
_____

MONDAY __ / __
_____
_____
_____
_____
_____

TUESDAY __ / __
_____
_____
_____
_____

WEDNESDAY __ / __
_____
_____
_____
_____

THURSDAY __ / __
_____
_____
_____
_____

FRIDAY __ / __
_____
_____
_____
_____

PLAYERS/TEAM PERFORMANCE

MATCH DETAILS

V

DATE

HOME/AWAY

RESULT

_____(Half time)_____

COMPETITION

WEATHER

PITCH

SCORERS (Times)

MATCH SUMMARY

PLAYERS/TEAM PERFORMANCE

MATCH DETAILS

V

DATE

HOME/AWAY

RESULT
_____ (Half time) _____

COMPETITION

WEATHER

PITCH

SCORERS (Times)

MATCH SUMMARY

> *'A match report on your opponents is a must. Telling your team not to worry about them is arrogant. Respect your opponents, but never be afraid of them – that's my motto.'*
> Eric Harrison

MY COACHING

What went well? _____

_____

What didn't? Why? _____

_____

What would I change next week? _____

_____

HANDLING OF THE MATCH

What went well? _____

_____

What didn't? Why? _____

_____

What changes would I make next week? _____

_____

IN GENERAL

List 3 positives from this week: _____

_____

What did I learn about coaching? _____

_____

What did I learn about myself? _____

_____

What two things will I work on next week? _____

_____

The biggest practice mistake is not to make a mistake

GOALS OF THE WEEK

TECHNICAL
_____
_____
_____

PHYSICAL
_____
_____
_____

TACTICAL
_____
_____
_____

MENTAL
_____
_____
_____

TEAM MEETINGS
_____
_____
_____
_____
_____
_____

MONDAY __ / __

TUESDAY __ / __

WEDNESDAY __ / __

THURSDAY __ / __

FRIDAY __ / __

PLAYERS/TEAM PERFORMANCE

MATCH DETAILS

V

DATE

HOME/AWAY

RESULT
_____ (Half time) _____

COMPETITION

WEATHER

PITCH

SCORERS (Times)

MATCH SUMMARY

PLAYERS/TEAM PERFORMANCE

MATCH DETAILS

V
_____

DATE
_____

HOME/AWAY
_____

RESULT
_____ (Half time) _____

COMPETITION
_____

WEATHER
_____

PITCH
_____

SCORERS (Times)

MATCH SUMMARY

> *'If you train badly, you play badly. If you work like a beast in training, you play the same way.'*
> Pep Guardiola

MY COACHING

What went well? _____
_____

What didn't? Why? _____
_____

What would I change next week? _____
_____

HANDLING OF THE MATCH

What went well? _____
_____

What didn't? Why? _____
_____

What changes would I make next week? _____
_____

IN GENERAL

List 3 positives from this week: _____
_____

What did I learn about coaching? _____
_____

What did I learn about myself? _____
_____

What two things will I work on next week? _____
_____

When things get complicated, go back to basics

GOALS OF THE WEEK

TECHNICAL

_____
_____

PHYSICAL

_____
_____

TACTICAL

_____
_____

MENTAL

_____
_____
_____

TEAM MEETINGS

_____
_____
_____
_____
_____
_____
_____
_____

MONDAY ___ / ___
_____
_____
_____
_____
_____

TUESDAY ___ / ___
_____
_____
_____
_____
_____

WEDNESDAY ___ / ___
_____
_____
_____
_____
_____

THURSDAY ___ / ___
_____
_____
_____
_____
_____

FRIDAY ___ / ___
_____
_____
_____
_____

PLAYERS/TEAM PERFORMANCE

MATCH DETAILS

V

DATE

HOME/AWAY

RESULT
_____ (Half time) _____

COMPETITION

WEATHER

PITCH

SCORERS (Times)

MATCH SUMMARY

MATCH DETAILS

V

DATE

HOME/AWAY

RESULT
_____ (Half time) _____

COMPETITION

WEATHER

PITCH

SCORERS (Times)

PLAYERS/TEAM PERFORMANCE

MATCH SUMMARY

> '*I love coaching players and keep trying to improve myself. Just like players, we coaches need to improve each day.*'
> Arsène Wenger

MY COACHING

What went well? _____

_____

What didn't? Why? _____

_____

What would I change next week? _____

_____

HANDLING OF THE MATCH(ES)

What went well? _____

_____

What didn't? Why? _____

_____

What changes would I make next week? _____

_____

IN GENERAL

List 3 positives from this week: _____

_____

What did I learn about coaching? _____

_____

What did I learn about myself? _____

_____

What two things will I work on next week? _____

_____

Coach through the game and in the game

GOALS OF THE WEEK

TECHNICAL

PHYSICAL

TACTICAL

MENTAL

TEAM MEETINGS

MONDAY   __ / __

TUESDAY   __ / __

WEDNESDAY   __ / __

THURSDAY   __ / __

FRIDAY   __ / __

MATCH DETAILS

V
_____

DATE
_____

HOME/AWAY
_____

RESULT
_____ (Half time) _____

COMPETITION
_____

WEATHER
_____

PITCH
_____

SCORERS (Times)
_____
_____
_____
_____

PLAYERS/TEAM PERFORMANCE

_____
_____
_____
_____
_____
_____
_____
_____
_____
_____
_____
_____
_____
_____
_____
_____
_____

MATCH SUMMARY

_____
_____
_____
_____
_____
_____
_____
_____
_____
_____

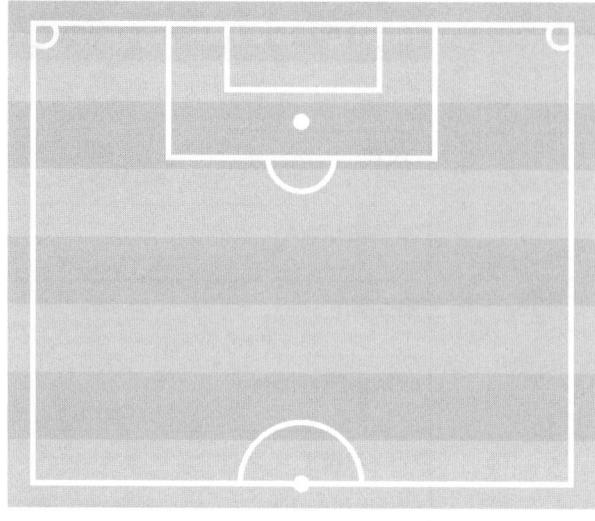

MATCH DETAILS

V

DATE

HOME/AWAY

RESULT
_____ (Half time) _____

COMPETITION

WEATHER

PITCH

SCORERS (Times)

PLAYERS/TEAM PERFORMANCE

MATCH SUMMARY

> *'There are scientists who will tell you that team spirit, because it can't be measured, doesn't exist. It does exist.'*
> Sam Allardyce

MY COACHING

What went well? _____
_____

What didn't? Why? _____
_____

What would I change next week? _____
_____

HANDLING OF THE MATCH

What went well? _____
_____

What didn't? Why? _____
_____

What changes would I make next week? _____
_____

IN GENERAL

List 3 positives from this week: _____
_____

What did I learn about coaching? _____
_____

What did I learn about myself? _____
_____

What two things will I work on next week? _____
_____

Remember each successful skill in the game needs a thousand reps in practice

GOALS OF THE WEEK

TECHNICAL

_____
_____
_____

PHYSICAL

_____
_____
_____

TACTICAL

_____
_____
_____

MENTAL

_____
_____
_____

TEAM MEETINGS

_____
_____
_____
_____
_____
_____
_____

MONDAY ___ / ___

TUESDAY ___ / ___

WEDNESDAY ___ / ___

THURSDAY ___ / ___

FRIDAY ___ / ___

PLAYERS/TEAM PERFORMANCE

MATCH DETAILS

V

DATE

HOME/AWAY

RESULT
_____ (Half time) _____

COMPETITION

WEATHER

PITCH

SCORERS (Times)

MATCH SUMMARY

PLAYERS/TEAM PERFORMANCE

MATCH DETAILS

V

DATE

HOME/AWAY

RESULT
_____ (Half time) _____

COMPETITION

WEATHER

PITCH

SCORERS (Times)

MATCH SUMMARY

> *'I don't know what happens on match day – the team is different to the one during the week. For whatever reason, the team does not perform anything like it does during practice.'*
> Sam Wyche

MY COACHING

What went well? _____

_____

What didn't? Why? _____

_____

What would I change next week? _____

_____

HANDLING OF THE MATCH(ES)

What went well? _____

_____

What didn't? Why? _____

_____

What changes would I make next week? _____

_____

IN GENERAL

List 3 positives from this week: _____

_____

What did I learn about coaching? _____

_____

What did I learn about myself? _____

_____

What two things will I work on next week? _____

_____

*Tough times don't last.
Tough teams do*

GOALS OF THE WEEK

TECHNICAL

PHYSICAL

TACTICAL

MENTAL

TEAM MEETINGS

MONDAY __ / __

TUESDAY __ / __

WEDNESDAY __ / __

THURSDAY __ / __

FRIDAY __ / __

PLAYERS/TEAM PERFORMANCE

MATCH DETAILS

V
_____

DATE
_____

HOME/AWAY
_____

RESULT
_____ (Half time) _____

COMPETITION
_____

WEATHER
_____

PITCH
_____

SCORERS (Times)

MATCH SUMMARY

PLAYERS/TEAM PERFORMANCE

MATCH DETAILS

V

DATE

HOME/AWAY

RESULT
_____ (Half time) _____

COMPETITION

WEATHER

PITCH

SCORERS (Times)

MATCH SUMMARY

> '*The world looks a totally different place after two wins.*'
> Gordon Strachan

MY COACHING

What went well? _____
_____

What didn't? Why? _____
_____

What would I change next week? _____
_____

HANDLING OF THE MATCH

What went well? _____
_____

What didn't? Why? _____
_____

What changes would I make next week? _____
_____

IN GENERAL

List 3 positives from this week: _____
_____

What did I learn about coaching? _____
_____

What did I learn about myself? _____
_____

What two things will I work on next week? _____
_____

If the team doesn't work together, it fails separately

GOALS OF THE WEEK

TECHNICAL

_____
_____
_____

PHYSICAL

_____
_____
_____

TACTICAL

_____
_____
_____

MENTAL

_____
_____
_____

TEAM MEETINGS

_____
_____
_____
_____
_____
_____
_____
_____

MONDAY   __ / __

TUESDAY   __ / __

WEDNESDAY   __ / __

THURSDAY   __ / __

FRIDAY   __ / __

MATCH DETAILS

V

DATE

HOME/AWAY

RESULT
_____ (Half time) _____

COMPETITION

WEATHER

PITCH

SCORERS (Times)

PLAYERS/TEAM PERFORMANCE

MATCH SUMMARY

PLAYERS/TEAM PERFORMANCE

MATCH DETAILS

V

DATE

HOME/AWAY

RESULT
_____ (Half time) _____

COMPETITION

WEATHER

PITCH

SCORERS (Times)

MATCH SUMMARY

> *'The importance of a good coach should never be underestimated, as a disorganised one has no chance. Coaches must look at themselves first.'*
> Eric Harrison

MY COACHING

What went well? _____

_____

What didn't? Why? _____

_____

What would I change next week? _____

_____

HANDLING OF THE MATCH(ES)

What went well? _____

_____

What didn't? Why? _____

_____

What changes would I make next week? _____

_____

IN GENERAL

List 3 positives from this week: _____

_____

What did I learn about coaching? _____

_____

What did I learn about myself? _____

_____

What two things will I work on next week? _____

_____

A win can often hide a multitude of sins in performance

GOALS OF THE WEEK

TECHNICAL

PHYSICAL

TACTICAL

MENTAL

TEAM MEETINGS

MONDAY __ / __

TUESDAY __ / __

WEDNESDAY __ / __

THURSDAY __ / __

FRIDAY __ / __

PLAYERS/TEAM PERFORMANCE

MATCH DETAILS

V

DATE

HOME/AWAY

RESULT
_____ (Half time) _____

COMPETITION

WEATHER

PITCH

SCORERS (Times)

MATCH SUMMARY

MATCH DETAILS

V

DATE

HOME/AWAY

RESULT
_____ (Half time) _____

COMPETITION

WEATHER

PITCH

SCORERS (Times)

PLAYERS/TEAM PERFORMANCE

MATCH SUMMARY

> *'Football is simple. You are in time or too late.*
> *When you are too late you should start sooner.'*
> Johan Cruyff

MY COACHING

What went well? _____
_____

What didn't? Why? _____
_____

What would I change next week? _____
_____

HANDLING OF THE MATCH(ES)

What went well? _____
_____

What didn't? Why? _____
_____

What changes would I make next week? _____
_____

IN GENERAL

List 3 positives from this week: _____
_____

What did I learn about coaching? _____
_____

What did I learn about myself? _____
_____

What two things will I work on next week? _____
_____

Say what you mean, and mean what you say

GOALS OF THE WEEK

TECHNICAL

PHYSICAL

TACTICAL

MENTAL

TEAM MEETINGS

MONDAY __ / __

TUESDAY __ / __

WEDNESDAY __ / __

THURSDAY __ / __

FRIDAY __ / __

PLAYERS/TEAM PERFORMANCE

MATCH DETAILS

V

DATE

HOME/AWAY

RESULT
_____(Half time)_____

COMPETITION

WEATHER

PITCH

SCORERS (Times)

MATCH SUMMARY

PLAYERS/TEAM PERFORMANCE

MATCH DETAILS

V

DATE

HOME/AWAY

RESULT

_____ (Half time) _____

COMPETITION

WEATHER

PITCH

SCORERS (Times)

MATCH SUMMARY

> '*Kids are brainwashed to play like robots – the natural way has been coached out of them. Over-coaching and no coaching are equally as bad – the coach must find the right balance.*'
> Brian Clough

MY COACHING

What went well? _____

_____

What didn't? Why? _____

_____

What would I change next week? _____

_____

HANDLING OF THE MATCH

What went well? _____

_____

What didn't? Why? _____

_____

What changes would I make next week? _____

_____

IN GENERAL

List 3 positives from this week: _____

_____

What did I learn about coaching? _____

_____

What did I learn about myself? _____

_____

What two things will I work on next week? _____

_____

A coach knows the way, goes the way, and shows the way

GOALS OF THE WEEK

TECHNICAL

_____
_____
_____

PHYSICAL

_____
_____
_____

TACTICAL

_____
_____
_____

MENTAL

_____
_____
_____

TEAM MEETINGS

_____
_____
_____
_____
_____
_____
_____

MONDAY __ / __

_____
_____
_____
_____
_____

TUESDAY __ / __

_____
_____
_____
_____
_____

WEDNESDAY __ / __

_____
_____
_____
_____
_____

THURSDAY __ / __

_____
_____
_____
_____
_____

FRIDAY __ / __

_____
_____
_____
_____
_____

PLAYERS/TEAM PERFORMANCE

MATCH DETAILS

V

DATE

HOME/AWAY

RESULT
_____ (Half time) _____

COMPETITION

WEATHER

PITCH

SCORERS (Times)

MATCH SUMMARY

PLAYERS/TEAM PERFORMANCE

MATCH DETAILS

V
_____

DATE
_____

HOME/AWAY
_____

RESULT
_____ (Half time) _____

COMPETITION
_____

WEATHER
_____

PITCH
_____

SCORERS (Times)

MATCH SUMMARY

> *'The individual character and quality of a coach can be seen the way he inspires his players – this can't be learned on a coaching course, only by life experience.'*
> Rinus Michels

MY COACHING

What went well? _____
_____

What didn't? Why? _____
_____

What would I change next week? _____
_____

HANDLING OF THE MATCH

What went well? _____
_____

What didn't? Why? _____
_____

What changes would I make next week?   _____
_____

IN GENERAL

List 3 positives from this week: _____
_____

What did I learn about coaching? _____
_____

What did I learn about myself? _____
_____

What two things will I work on next week? _____
_____

A coach must risk defeat in search of victory

GOALS OF THE WEEK

TECHNICAL
_____
_____
_____

PHYSICAL
_____
_____
_____

TACTICAL
_____
_____
_____

MENTAL
_____
_____
_____

TEAM MEETINGS
_____
_____
_____
_____
_____
_____
_____

MONDAY ___ / ___

TUESDAY ___ / ___

WEDNESDAY ___ / ___

THURSDAY ___ / ___

FRIDAY ___ / ___

MATCH DETAILS

V

DATE

HOME/AWAY

RESULT
_____ (Half time) _____

COMPETITION

WEATHER

PITCH

SCORERS (Times)

PLAYERS/TEAM PERFORMANCE

MATCH SUMMARY

MATCH DETAILS

V

DATE

HOME/AWAY

RESULT
_____ (Half time) _____

COMPETITION

WEATHER

PITCH

SCORERS (Times)

PLAYERS/TEAM PERFORMANCE

MATCH SUMMARY

> 'Tactical things are so important, you cannot win without tactics, but the emotion makes the difference.'
> Jürgen Klopp

MY COACHING

What went well? _____

_____

What didn't? Why? _____

_____

What would I change next week? _____

_____

HANDLING OF THE MATCH

What went well? _____

_____

What didn't? Why? _____

_____

What changes would I make next week? _____

_____

IN GENERAL

List 3 positives from this week: _____

_____

What did I learn about coaching? _____

_____

What did I learn about myself? _____

_____

What two things will I work on next week? _____

_____

> *When you make a big decision today, think of its consequences tomorrow*

GOALS OF THE WEEK

TECHNICAL
_____
_____
_____

PHYSICAL
_____
_____
_____

TACTICAL
_____
_____
_____

MENTAL
_____
_____
_____

TEAM MEETINGS
_____
_____
_____
_____
_____
_____
_____

MONDAY ___ / ___
_____
_____
_____
_____
_____

TUESDAY ___ / ___
_____
_____
_____
_____

WEDNESDAY ___ / ___
_____
_____
_____
_____

THURSDAY ___ / ___
_____
_____
_____
_____
_____

FRIDAY ___ / ___
_____
_____
_____
_____
_____

MATCH DETAILS

V

DATE

HOME/AWAY

RESULT
_____ (Half time) _____

COMPETITION

WEATHER

PITCH

SCORERS (Times)

PLAYERS/TEAM PERFORMANCE

MATCH SUMMARY

MATCH DETAILS

V

DATE

HOME/AWAY

RESULT
_____ (Half time) _____

COMPETITION

WEATHER

PITCH

SCORERS (Times)

PLAYERS/TEAM PERFORMANCE

MATCH SUMMARY

'Too many coaches use activities that keep kids entertained but do nil for their learning. If a coach is in doubt what to do, use small-sided games.'
Rinus Michel

MY COACHING

What went well? _____
_____

What didn't? Why? _____
_____

What would I change next week? _____
_____

HANDLING OF THE MATCH

What went well? _____
_____

What didn't? Why? _____
_____

What changes would I make next week? _____
_____

IN GENERAL

List 3 positives from this week: _____
_____

What did I learn about coaching? _____
_____

What did I learn about myself? _____
_____

What two things will I work on next week? _____
_____

*The approach
should always be:
one step at a time*

GOALS OF THE WEEK

TECHNICAL

_____
_____
_____

PHYSICAL

_____
_____
_____

TACTICAL

_____
_____
_____

MENTAL

_____
_____
_____

TEAM MEETINGS

_____
_____
_____
_____
_____
_____
_____
_____

MONDAY __ / __

TUESDAY __ / __

WEDNESDAY __ / __

THURSDAY __ / __

FRIDAY __ / __

PLAYERS/TEAM PERFORMANCE

MATCH DETAILS

V

DATE

HOME/AWAY

RESULT
_____ (Half time) _____

COMPETITION

WEATHER

PITCH

SCORERS (Times)

MATCH SUMMARY

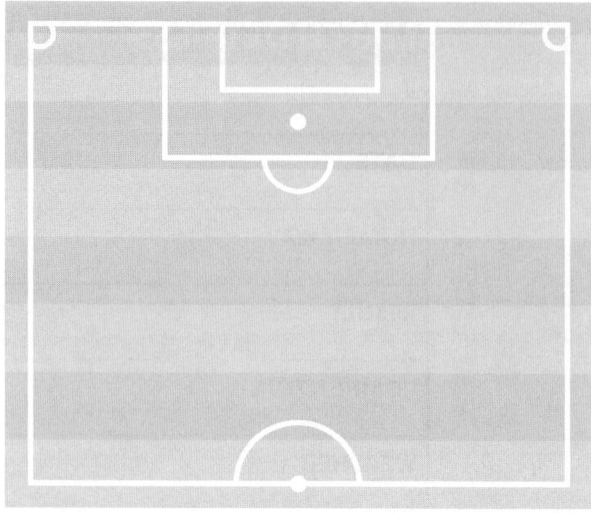

MATCH DETAILS

V
_____

DATE
_____

HOME/AWAY
_____

RESULT
_____ (Half time) _____

COMPETITION
_____

WEATHER
_____

PITCH
_____

SCORERS (Times)
_____
_____
_____
_____

PLAYERS/TEAM PERFORMANCE

_____
_____
_____
_____
_____
_____
_____
_____
_____
_____
_____
_____
_____
_____
_____
_____
_____

MATCH SUMMARY

_____
_____
_____
_____
_____
_____
_____
_____
_____
_____

> *'Young players should have the freedom to play without numbers on their shirts, set roles or fixed positions. They will sort it out if allowed to – no shouting, instructing or "one-touch".'*
> Vincenzo Chiarenza

MY COACHING

What went well? _____
_____

What didn't? Why? _____
_____

What would I change next week? _____
_____

HANDLING OF THE MATCH

What went well? _____
_____

What didn't? Why? _____
_____

What changes would I make next week?   _____
_____

IN GENERAL

List 3 positives from this week: _____
_____

What did I learn about coaching? _____
_____

What did I learn about myself? _____
_____

What two things will I work on next week? _____
_____

Don't fear failure when you try something new

GOALS OF THE WEEK

TECHNICAL
_____
_____
_____

PHYSICAL
_____
_____
_____

TACTICAL
_____
_____
_____

MENTAL
_____
_____
_____

TEAM MEETINGS
_____
_____
_____
_____
_____
_____
_____

MONDAY __ / __
_____
_____
_____
_____
_____

TUESDAY __ / __
_____
_____
_____
_____
_____

WEDNESDAY __ / __
_____
_____
_____
_____
_____

THURSDAY __ / __
_____
_____
_____
_____
_____

FRIDAY __ / __
_____
_____
_____
_____
_____

MATCH DETAILS

V

DATE

HOME/AWAY

RESULT
_____ (Half time) _____

COMPETITION

WEATHER

PITCH

SCORERS (Times)

PLAYERS/TEAM PERFORMANCE

MATCH SUMMARY

PLAYERS/TEAM PERFORMANCE

MATCH DETAILS

V

DATE

HOME/AWAY

RESULT
_____ (Half time) _____

COMPETITION

WEATHER

PITCH

SCORERS (Times)

MATCH SUMMARY

> *'Coaches best develop players through small-sided games where they can manipulate the practice to increase their game understanding without having to dictate every move to them.'*
> Horst Wein

MY COACHING

What went well? _____
_____

What didn't? Why? _____
_____

What would I change next week? _____
_____

HANDLING OF THE MATCH

What went well? _____
_____

What didn't? Why? _____
_____

What changes would I make next week? _____
_____

IN GENERAL

List 3 positives from this week: _____
_____

What did I learn about coaching? _____
_____

What did I learn about myself? _____
_____

What two things will I work on next week? _____
_____

With commitment there are only two options: either you're in or you're out. There's no in between

GOALS OF THE WEEK

TECHNICAL

_____
_____

PHYSICAL

_____
_____

TACTICAL

_____
_____

MENTAL

_____
_____
_____

TEAM MEETINGS

_____
_____
_____
_____
_____
_____
_____

MONDAY __ / __

TUESDAY __ / __

WEDNESDAY __ / __

THURSDAY __ / __

FRIDAY __ / __

PLAYERS/TEAM PERFORMANCE

MATCH DETAILS

V

DATE

HOME/AWAY

RESULT
_____(Half time)_____

COMPETITION

WEATHER

PITCH

SCORERS (Times)

MATCH SUMMARY

PLAYERS/TEAM PERFORMANCE

MATCH DETAILS

V

DATE

HOME/AWAY

RESULT
_____ (Half time) _____

COMPETITION

WEATHER

PITCH

SCORERS (Times)

MATCH SUMMARY

> 'Coaches must learn to stay calm. I do this through experience and always check my mental state before the game. Am I nervous or angry today? I need to be sure that I can cope with the situation.'
>
> Arsène Wenger

MY COACHING

What went well? _____

_____

What didn't? Why? _____

_____

What would I change next week? _____

_____

HANDLING OF THE MATCH

What went well? _____

_____

What didn't? Why? _____

_____

What changes would I make next week? _____

_____

IN GENERAL

List 3 positives from this week: _____

_____

What did I learn about coaching? _____

_____

What did I learn about myself? _____

_____

What two things will I work on next week? _____

_____

You have not coached until they have actually learned

GOALS OF THE WEEK

TECHNICAL

_____

_____

_____

PHYSICAL

_____

_____

_____

TACTICAL

_____

_____

_____

MENTAL

_____

_____

_____

TEAM MEETINGS

_____

_____

_____

_____

_____

_____

_____

_____

MONDAY ___ / ___

TUESDAY ___ / ___

WEDNESDAY ___ / ___

THURSDAY ___ / ___

FRIDAY ___ / ___

PLAYERS/TEAM PERFORMANCE

MATCH DETAILS

V

DATE

HOME/AWAY

RESULT
_____ (Half time) _____

COMPETITION

WEATHER

PITCH

SCORERS (Times)

MATCH SUMMARY

PLAYERS/TEAM PERFORMANCE

MATCH DETAILS

V

DATE

HOME/AWAY

RESULT
_____ (Half time) _____

COMPETITION

WEATHER

PITCH

SCORERS (Times)

MATCH SUMMARY

> *'Don't be over-critical of players' weaknesses – proceed with caution. Sympathize with ones who work on their problems, but not with those who bring about their own downfall by selfish play, poor attitude or who ignore good advice.'*
> Pat Welton

MY COACHING

What went well? _____

_____

What didn't? Why? _____

_____

What would I change next week? _____

_____

HANDLING OF THE MATCH

What went well? _____

_____

What didn't? Why? _____

_____

What changes would I make next week? _____

_____

IN GENERAL

List 3 positives from this week: _____

_____

What did I learn about coaching? _____

_____

What did I learn about myself? _____

_____

What two things will I work on next week? _____

_____

*Failure is success if
we learn from it*

GOALS OF THE WEEK

TECHNICAL
_____
_____
_____

PHYSICAL
_____
_____
_____

TACTICAL
_____
_____
_____

MENTAL
_____
_____
_____

TEAM MEETINGS
_____
_____
_____
_____
_____
_____
_____

MONDAY ___ / ___
_____
_____
_____
_____
_____

TUESDAY ___ / ___
_____
_____
_____
_____

WEDNESDAY ___ / ___
_____
_____
_____
_____

THURSDAY ___ / ___
_____
_____
_____
_____

FRIDAY ___ / ___
_____
_____
_____
_____

PLAYERS/TEAM PERFORMANCE

MATCH DETAILS

V

DATE

HOME/AWAY

RESULT
_____ (Half time) _____

COMPETITION

WEATHER

PITCH

SCORERS (Times)

MATCH SUMMARY

MATCH DETAILS

V

DATE

HOME/AWAY

RESULT
_____ (Half time) _____

COMPETITION

WEATHER

PITCH

SCORERS (Times)

PLAYERS/TEAM PERFORMANCE

MATCH SUMMARY

> *'I will forgive if the players cannot get it right,
> but not if they do not try hard.'*
> Pep Guardiola

MY COACHING

What went well? _____
_____

What didn't? Why? _____
_____

What would I change next week? _____
_____

HANDLING OF THE MATCH

What went well? _____
_____

What didn't? Why? _____
_____

What changes would I make next week? _____
_____

IN GENERAL

List 3 positives from this week: _____
_____

What did I learn about coaching? _____
_____

What did I learn about myself? _____
_____

What two things will I work on next week? _____
_____

TEAM REALITY CHECK

PURPOSE

To provide an accurate profile of the team's current abilities.

FACTOR RATING SCALE

DATE ASSESSED __ / __ / ____

KEY FACTORS	VERY LOW 1–2	LOW 3–4	AVERAGE 5–6	HIGH 7–8	VERY HIGH 9–10
1 DISCIPLINE					
2 TECHNICAL					
3 CONCENTRATION					
4 COACHABILITY					
5 TACTICAL					
6 LEADERSHIP					
7 FITNESS					
8 TEAMWORK					
9 CONFIDENCE					
10 DETERMINATION					

HOW TO DO IT

1. Read the Key Team Factors (page 8) so you understand them. Rate each one honestly and mark with a highlighter pen to produce a visual graph/profile of your team.

2. For more accuracy, get your coaches and/or players to complete a 'team reality check' sheet. Compare the results with your own and discuss differences with them until a score is agreed on.

*Be a winner in
football and in life*

GOALS OF THE WEEK

TECHNICAL
_____
_____

PHYSICAL
_____
_____

TACTICAL
_____
_____

MENTAL
_____
_____
_____

TEAM MEETINGS
_____
_____
_____
_____
_____
_____
_____

MONDAY __ / __
_____
_____
_____
_____

TUESDAY __ / __
_____
_____
_____
_____

WEDNESDAY __ / __
_____
_____
_____
_____

THURSDAY __ / __
_____
_____
_____
_____

FRIDAY __ / __
_____
_____
_____
_____

MATCH DETAILS

V
_____

DATE
_____

HOME/AWAY
_____

RESULT
_____(Half time)_____

COMPETITION
_____

WEATHER
_____

PITCH
_____

SCORERS (Times)
_____
_____
_____
_____

PLAYERS/TEAM PERFORMANCE

_____
_____
_____
_____
_____
_____
_____
_____
_____
_____
_____
_____
_____
_____
_____
_____
_____

MATCH SUMMARY

_____
_____
_____
_____
_____
_____
_____
_____
_____

MATCH DETAILS

V

DATE

HOME/AWAY

RESULT
_____ (Half time) _____

COMPETITION

WEATHER

PITCH

SCORERS (Times)

PLAYERS/TEAM PERFORMANCE

MATCH SUMMARY

'To be the ultimate team, you must use your body and your mind. Draw up on the resources of your teammates. Choose your steps wisely and you will win. Remember only teams succeed.'
Jose Mourinho

MY COACHING

What went well? _____

_____

What didn't? Why? _____

_____

What would I change next week? _____

_____

HANDLING OF THE MATCH

What went well? _____

_____

What didn't? Why? _____

_____

What changes would I make next week? _____

_____

IN GENERAL

List 3 positives from this week: _____

_____

What did I learn about coaching? _____

_____

What did I learn about myself? _____

_____

What two things will I work on next week? _____

_____

Remember, you're not totally responsible when the team wins, nor when it loses

GOALS OF THE WEEK

TECHNICAL
_____
_____
_____

PHYSICAL
_____
_____
_____

TACTICAL
_____
_____
_____

MENTAL
_____
_____
_____

TEAM MEETINGS
_____
_____
_____
_____
_____
_____
_____

MONDAY __ / __
_____
_____
_____
_____
_____
_____

TUESDAY __ / __
_____
_____
_____
_____
_____

WEDNESDAY __ / __
_____
_____
_____
_____
_____

THURSDAY __ / __
_____
_____
_____
_____
_____

FRIDAY __ / __
_____
_____
_____
_____

MATCH DETAILS

V

DATE

HOME/AWAY

RESULT
_____ (Half time) _____

COMPETITION

WEATHER

PITCH

SCORERS (Times)

PLAYERS/TEAM PERFORMANCE

MATCH SUMMARY

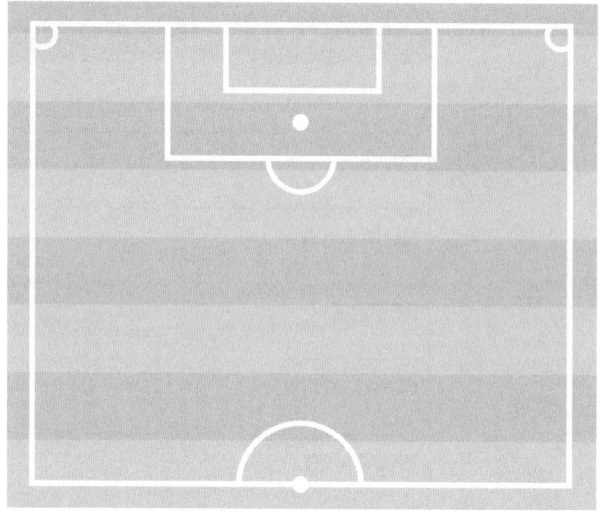

PLAYERS/TEAM PERFORMANCE

MATCH DETAILS

V

DATE

HOME/AWAY

RESULT
_____ (Half time) _____

COMPETITION

WEATHER

PITCH

SCORERS (Times)

MATCH SUMMARY

> *'You need determination as a coach. If you come in on Monday morning after a defeat without "fire in your belly", it will show to your players.'*
> Sir Alex Ferguson

MY COACHING

What went well? _____

_____

What didn't? Why? _____

_____

What would I change next week? _____

_____

HANDLING OF THE MATCH

What went well? _____

_____

What didn't? Why? _____

_____

What changes would I make next week? _____

_____

IN GENERAL

List 3 positives from this week: _____

_____

What did I learn about coaching? _____

_____

What did I learn about myself? _____

_____

What two things will I work on next week? _____

_____

Coaches and players want 3 things from the game: to compete, to improve, and to win

GOALS OF THE WEEK

TECHNICAL

PHYSICAL

TACTICAL

MENTAL

TEAM MEETINGS

MONDAY ___ / ___

TUESDAY ___ / ___

WEDNESDAY ___ / ___

THURSDAY ___ / ___

FRIDAY ___ / ___

MATCH DETAILS

V

DATE

HOME/AWAY

RESULT
_____ (Half time) _____

COMPETITION

WEATHER

PITCH

SCORERS (Times)

PLAYERS/TEAM PERFORMANCE

MATCH SUMMARY

MATCH DETAILS

V

_____

DATE

_____

HOME/AWAY

_____

RESULT

_____ (Half time) _____

COMPETITION

_____

WEATHER

_____

PITCH

_____

SCORERS (Times)

_____

_____

_____

_____

PLAYERS/TEAM PERFORMANCE

_____
_____
_____
_____
_____
_____
_____
_____
_____
_____
_____
_____
_____
_____
_____

MATCH SUMMARY

_____
_____
_____
_____
_____
_____
_____
_____
_____
_____

> *'I learned much from my coach about my game. We always worked on the part of the pitch where I played so it became second nature. I loved practice, unlike others who just wanted to play.'*
> Tony Adams

MY COACHING

What went well? _____
_____

What didn't? Why? _____
_____

What would I change next week? _____
_____

HANDLING OF THE MATCH

What went well? _____
_____

What didn't? Why? _____
_____

What changes would I make next week? _____
_____

IN GENERAL

List 3 positives from this week: _____
_____

What did I learn about coaching? _____
_____

What did I learn about myself? _____
_____

What two things will I work on next week? _____
_____

*Behind most
successful teams there
is a talented coach*

GOALS OF THE WEEK

TECHNICAL

_____
_____
_____

PHYSICAL

_____
_____
_____

TACTICAL

_____
_____
_____

MENTAL

_____
_____
_____

TEAM MEETINGS

_____
_____
_____
_____
_____
_____
_____

MONDAY   __ / __

TUESDAY   __ / __

WEDNESDAY   __ / __

THURSDAY   __ / __

FRIDAY   __ / __

PLAYERS/TEAM PERFORMANCE

MATCH DETAILS

V

DATE

HOME/AWAY

RESULT
_____ (Half time) _____

COMPETITION

WEATHER

PITCH

SCORERS (Times)

MATCH SUMMARY

MATCH DETAILS

V

DATE

HOME/AWAY

RESULT
_____ (Half time) _____

COMPETITION

WEATHER

PITCH

SCORERS (Times)

PLAYERS/TEAM PERFORMANCE

MATCH SUMMARY

> *'Good communication is important. I see sessions where the coach talks to the player but the message does not arrive. Remember when you were a player, standing in the cold as the coach rambled on, when you just wanted to play? Don't over-talk.'*
> Sir Alex Ferguson

MY COACHING

What went well? _____
_____

What didn't? Why? _____
_____

What would I change next week? _____
_____

HANDLING OF THE MATCH

What went well? _____
_____

What didn't? Why? _____
_____

What changes would I make next week? _____
_____

IN GENERAL

List 3 positives from this week: _____
_____

What did I learn about coaching? _____
_____

What did I learn about myself? _____
_____

What two things will I work on next week? _____
_____

Football is a simple game, sometimes made difficult by coaches

GOALS OF THE WEEK

TECHNICAL
_____
_____
_____

PHYSICAL
_____
_____
_____

TACTICAL
_____
_____
_____

MENTAL
_____
_____
_____

TEAM MEETINGS
_____
_____
_____
_____
_____
_____
_____

MONDAY   __ / __
_____
_____
_____
_____

TUESDAY   __ / __
_____
_____
_____
_____

WEDNESDAY   __ / __
_____
_____
_____
_____

THURSDAY   __ / __
_____
_____
_____
_____

FRIDAY   __ / __
_____
_____
_____
_____

PLAYERS/TEAM PERFORMANCE

MATCH DETAILS

V
_____

DATE
_____

HOME/AWAY
_____

RESULT
_____ (Half time) _____

COMPETITION
_____

WEATHER
_____

PITCH
_____

SCORERS (Times)
_____
_____
_____
_____

MATCH SUMMARY

MATCH DETAILS

V

DATE

HOME/AWAY

RESULT
_____ (Half time) _____

COMPETITION

WEATHER

PITCH

SCORERS (Times)

PLAYERS/TEAM PERFORMANCE

MATCH SUMMARY

> *'I coach by asking questions: "What should we do here?" or "How can we solve the problem?" By asking them, you will make them become thinking players.'*
> Rafael Benitez

MY COACHING

What went well? _____
_____

What didn't? Why? _____
_____

What would I change next week? _____
_____

HANDLING OF THE MATCH

What went well? _____
_____

What didn't? Why? _____
_____

What changes would I make next week? _____
_____

IN GENERAL

List 3 positives from this week: _____
_____

What did I learn about coaching? _____
_____

What did I learn about myself? _____
_____

What two things will I work on next week? _____
_____

*Problems are the price
you pay for success*

GOALS OF THE WEEK

TECHNICAL

_____

_____

_____

PHYSICAL

_____

_____

_____

TACTICAL

_____

_____

_____

MENTAL

_____

_____

_____

TEAM MEETINGS

_____

_____

_____

_____

_____

_____

_____

_____

MONDAY ___ / ___

TUESDAY ___ / ___

WEDNESDAY ___ / ___

THURSDAY ___ / ___

FRIDAY ___ / ___

MATCH DETAILS

V

DATE

HOME/AWAY

RESULT
_____ (Half time) _____

COMPETITION

WEATHER

PITCH

SCORERS (Times)

PLAYERS/TEAM PERFORMANCE

MATCH SUMMARY

MATCH DETAILS

V

DATE

HOME/AWAY

RESULT
_____ (Half time) _____

COMPETITION

WEATHER

PITCH

SCORERS (Times)

PLAYERS/TEAM PERFORMANCE

MATCH SUMMARY

> *'I prefer a "guided discovery" approach with feedback from the players. At times, practice starts one way and ends in a different direction. The days of "just do as I say" for the coach are long gone.'*
> José Mourinho

MY COACHING

What went well? _____
_____

What didn't? Why? _____

What would I change next week? _____
_____

HANDLING OF THE MATCH

What went well? _____
_____

What didn't? Why? _____
_____

What changes would I make next week? _____
_____

IN GENERAL

List 3 positives from this week: _____
_____

What did I learn about coaching? _____
_____

What did I learn about myself? _____
_____

What two things will I work on next week? _____
_____

Coach, today's goals can be tomorrow's realities

GOALS OF THE WEEK

TECHNICAL

_____
_____
_____

PHYSICAL

_____
_____
_____

TACTICAL

_____
_____
_____

MENTAL

_____
_____
_____

TEAM MEETINGS

_____
_____
_____
_____
_____
_____
_____

MONDAY __ / __

TUESDAY __ / __

WEDNESDAY __ / __

THURSDAY __ / __

FRIDAY __ / __

PLAYERS/TEAM PERFORMANCE

MATCH DETAILS

V

DATE

HOME/AWAY

RESULT
_____ (Half time) _____

COMPETITION

WEATHER

PITCH

SCORERS (Times)

MATCH SUMMARY

PLAYERS/TEAM PERFORMANCE

MATCH DETAILS

V

DATE

HOME/AWAY

RESULT
_____ (Half time) _____

COMPETITION

WEATHER

PITCH

SCORERS (Times)

MATCH SUMMARY

> 'We do all our practice sessions on two pitches alongside each other, which lets us plan better and stop us having to move equipment about. We move from pitch to pitch, taking fluid in between.'
> José Mourinho

MY COACHING

What went well? _____
_____

What didn't? Why? _____
_____

What would I change next week? _____
_____

HANDLING OF THE MATCH

What went well? _____
_____

What didn't? Why? _____
_____

What changes would I make next week? _____
_____

IN GENERAL

List 3 positives from this week: _____
_____

What did I learn about coaching? _____
_____

What did I learn about myself? _____
_____

What two things will I work on next week? _____
_____

Make something good out of something bad

GOALS OF THE WEEK

TECHNICAL

PHYSICAL

TACTICAL

MENTAL

TEAM MEETINGS

MONDAY __ / __

TUESDAY __ / __

WEDNESDAY __ / __

THURSDAY __ / __

FRIDAY __ / __

PLAYERS/TEAM PERFORMANCE

MATCH DETAILS

V
_____

DATE
_____

HOME/AWAY
_____

RESULT
_____ (Half time) _____

COMPETITION
_____

WEATHER
_____

PITCH
_____

SCORERS (Times)
_____
_____
_____
_____

MATCH SUMMARY

PLAYERS/TEAM PERFORMANCE

MATCH DETAILS

V

DATE

HOME/AWAY

RESULT
_____ (Half time) _____

COMPETITION

WEATHER

PITCH

SCORERS (Times)

MATCH SUMMARY

> 'I use the word "why" to show how coaching has changed. Today's players want to know the reasons for every session – as coach, you need to know the answer.'
> Gérard Houllier

MY COACHING

What went well? _____
_____

What didn't? Why? _____
_____

What would I change next week? _____
_____

HANDLING OF THE MATCH

What went well? _____
_____

What didn't? Why? _____
_____

What changes would I make next week? _____
_____

IN GENERAL

List 3 positives from this week: _____
_____

What did I learn about coaching? _____
_____

What did I learn about myself? _____
_____

What two things will I work on next week? _____
_____

Pressure is often something we put on ourselves

GOALS OF THE WEEK

TECHNICAL

_____
_____
_____

PHYSICAL

_____
_____
_____

TACTICAL

_____
_____
_____

MENTAL

_____
_____
_____

TEAM MEETINGS

_____
_____
_____
_____
_____
_____
_____

MONDAY   __ / __

TUESDAY   __ / __

WEDNESDAY   __ / __

THURSDAY   __ / __

FRIDAY   __ / __

PLAYERS/TEAM PERFORMANCE

MATCH DETAILS

V

DATE

HOME/AWAY

RESULT
_____(Half time)_____

COMPETITION

WEATHER

PITCH

SCORERS (Times)

MATCH SUMMARY

PLAYERS/TEAM PERFORMANCE

MATCH DETAILS

V
_____

DATE
_____

HOME/AWAY
_____

RESULT
_____ (Half time) _____

COMPETITION
_____

WEATHER
_____

PITCH
_____

SCORERS (Times)
_____
_____
_____
_____

MATCH SUMMARY

> *'Coach, when you are older, you can either say you know it all or still have much to learn. When I was younger, I tried to pump all my knowledge into players fast – big mistake! Now I do it bit-by-bit. Wish I had known this sooner.'*
> Foppe de Haan

MY COACHING

What went well? _____
_____

What didn't? Why? _____
_____

What would I change next week? _____
_____

HANDLING OF THE MATCH

What went well? _____
_____

What didn't? Why? _____
_____

What changes would I make next week? _____
_____

IN GENERAL

List 3 positives from this week: _____
_____

What did I learn about coaching? _____
_____

What did I learn about myself? _____
_____

What two things will I work on next week? _____
_____

Don't let mistakes get you down – every one is another step up

GOALS OF THE WEEK

TECHNICAL

_____
_____
_____

PHYSICAL

_____
_____
_____

TACTICAL

_____
_____
_____

MENTAL

_____
_____
_____

TEAM MEETINGS

_____
_____
_____
_____
_____
_____
_____

MONDAY ___ / ___

_____
_____
_____
_____
_____

TUESDAY ___ / ___

_____
_____
_____
_____

WEDNESDAY ___ / ___

_____
_____
_____
_____

THURSDAY ___ / ___

_____
_____
_____
_____

FRIDAY ___ / ___

_____
_____
_____
_____

MATCH DETAILS

V
_____

DATE
_____

HOME/AWAY
_____

RESULT
_____ (Half time) _____

COMPETITION
_____

WEATHER
_____

PITCH
_____

SCORERS (Times)
_____
_____
_____
_____

PLAYERS/TEAM PERFORMANCE

MATCH SUMMARY

PLAYERS/TEAM PERFORMANCE

MATCH DETAILS

V

DATE

HOME/AWAY

RESULT
_____ (Half time) _____

COMPETITION

WEATHER

PITCH

SCORERS (Times)

MATCH SUMMARY

'If you do not believe you can do it
then you have no chance at all.'
Arsène Wenger

MY COACHING

What went well? _____
_____

What didn't? Why? _____
_____

What would I change next week? _____
_____

HANDLING OF THE MATCH

What went well? _____
_____

What didn't? Why? _____
_____

What changes would I make next week? _____
_____

IN GENERAL

List 3 positives from this week: _____
_____

What did I learn about coaching? _____
_____

What did I learn about myself? _____
_____

What two things will I work on next week? _____
_____

CLOSE SEASON

> *Many unknown factors can hit you during the playing season, so planning is essential. We start in the summer before the ball is kicked. As soon as the new fixture list is out, we go over it to study travel distances, likely weather, competitions, opponents and all the relevant details. We try to rearrange fixtures/details when there are heavy demands on the team – nothing is left to chance. By anticipating problems before they arise, you are not breaking rules or taking an unfair advantage, just being professional.*

Bob Paisley

PURPOSE

To gather data from the season that's just gone, which lets us learn and start our planning and preparation for the coming playing season.

1. EVALUATION

Assess all the key factors related to the team's total performance over the season. Obtain information from your players, staff or anyone else who can assist. Get feedback from match and/or training reports, statistics, small meetings, video analysis, etc. Valuable lessons must be learned and acted upon for next season!

2. RECOVERY

Everyone needs a break to charge their batteries after the season. However, too much inactivity can cause a fitness decline, which puts players at a disadvantage when they arrive back for the pre-season training. Set players' goals to focus on, to prevent over-eating or drinking and ensure that they maintain an appropriate body weight.

3. PLANNING

It is now the end of the old season, but the coach's work is never done! Get a break, but look to get a head start over your opponents with your early planning and preparation at this quiet time of the season. It will save you, your team and staff much time, effort and frustration when the new season gets under way.

TEAM REALITY CHECK

PURPOSE

To provide an accurate profile of the team's current abilities at the end of the season.

FACTOR RATING SCALE

DATE ASSESSED __ / __ / _____

KEY FACTORS	VERY LOW 1–2	LOW 3–4	AVERAGE 5–6	HIGH 7–8	VERY HIGH 9–10
1 DISCIPLINE					
2 TECHNICAL					
3 CONCENTRATION					
4 COACHABILITY					
5 TACTICAL					
6 LEADERSHIP					
7 FITNESS					
8 TEAMWORK					
9 CONFIDENCE					
10 DETERMINATION					

HOW TO DO IT

1. Read the Key Team Factors (page 8) so you understand them. Rate each one honestly and mark with a highlighter pen to produce a visual graph/profile of your team.

2. For more accuracy, get your coaches and/or players to complete a 'team reality check' sheet. Compare the results with your own and discuss differences with them until a score is agreed on.

PLAYER STATISTICS

DATE ASSESSED _ _ / _ _ / _ _ _ _

N°	NAMES	N° OF APPEARANCES	N° OF TIMES SUBSTITUTED	N° OF TIMES INJURED	GOALS SCORED	GOAL ASSISTS	GOAL SHUT-OUTS (GK)	YELLOW CARDS	RED CARDS	COMMENTS
1										
2										
3										
4										
5										
6										
7										
8										
9										
10										
11										
12										
13										
14										
15										
16										
17										
18										
19										
20										
21										
22										
23										
24										

THE SEASON REVIEW

This is the starting point for the new season. Everyone needs a rest to recover and recharge their physical, mental and emotional batteries for the approaching season however, it is a valuable time to reflect on what you have done over the season just gone.

By gathering, analysing and using vital information it can gain you an advantage over your rivals, and by assessing the season more objectively you can see some of the positive or negative patterns that have emerged, allowing you as coach to do something about them.

Areas that could be reviewed include:

COACHING AND TRAINING

The quality

The actual programme contents

The communication

The players response

The warm-up/cool-down

MATCH PERFORMANCE

Defending and attacking

Set-plays

System of play

Tactics used

The pre-match preparation

Feedback of players

TEAM MEETINGS

How many?

Too much or too little?

How effective?

What needs changing?

PLAYERS

Match appearances

Overall performance

Injuries

Substitutions

Cautions

Goals and assists

Each coach can decide the factors that are important. In a nutshell, he can decide on what went well and what didn't and revise this planning for the forthcoming season on that basis.

Remember to get your planner for the new season!

Good luck!